UNDER THE COVER

A MEMOIR

Herklee Hubbard, Jr.

UNDER THE COVER

A MEMOIR

Under the Cover, LLC
Copyright © 2022 Herklee Hubbard, Jr.

All rights reserved. No part of this publication may be reproduced or transmitted in any form or by any means without the written permission of the publisher. All rights reserved.

ISBN: 978-1-956884-05-0

Contributing Editor: or all services completed
by Imprint Productions, Inc.
Cover Design: or all services completed
by Imprint Productions, Inc.

Printed in the United States of America
Published by Imprint Productions, Inc.
First Edition 2022

I dedicate this memoir to the memory of my beloved wife, Ocella Hubbard. I miss you dearly.

And also to my parents, the late Mr. and Mrs. Herklee and Mary Hubbard, Sr., and my siblings; Johnny, Ernest, Henry, Charlie, Ervin, Willie, Katherine, John, James, Simon, and Julia. To my children; Robert, Charlene, Herklee III, Keith, and Tyrone, and all of my grandkids, nephews, nieces, cousins, friends, and loved ones. I wrote this for you. I've included some fun times memories at the back of the memoir of family and friends. Thank you, and enjoy these memories with me.

INTRODUCTION

As I reminisce over the early years of my life, there were many experiences, memories and reflections that happened back then that are very much a part of the fascinating life I have lived. Life today is starkly different from the strict and disciplined upbring of my siblings and I. Being raised with both parents that were serious about the chores and responsibilities they assigned to me and my

11 siblings, help make me the man I became. What was fun for us back in the day doesn't even exist for the kids today. Although we didn't have the kind of accessibility to education, money, clothing, cars, and material things as the kids have today, we had good wholesome fun that didn't cost half of what it costs to entertain the kids today.

Well, buckle up cause I'll share some things that will make you laugh, cry, or even mad. Enjoy the memories and know that I'm grateful to be 92 years old, have an active mind, enjoying my retired life as a father, and grandfather to my children.

There were twelve children born to Herklee and Mary Hubbard Sr. As far as I can recollect, it all started back in the 30s in Houston County, Georgia where we lived on a plantation. I remember one winter, when some of us were small, our mom got sick with the flu and stayed in bed. I can't remember what year it was, but all the kids were sick, including the baby at the time. We all had all kinds of childhood diseases and the only one who was not ill was dad. He had to come in from plowing and fix all of us food. Being stuck in bed was the worst thing I can remember as a child. When night came, daddy had to come home to cut enough wood to last through the night and into the next day. After that, he would prepare food for those that could eat, but Mom could hardly eat. She ate just enough to make milk to nurse the baby.

In those days, we didn't have vaccinations, we depended wholly on God. He brought us through everything, we didn't know what a doctor was. We used home remedies and prayed to the Lord that we would get well. Don't forget about Castor oil, back then people used Castor oil for everything. Back then we used sardines to rub with the oil, and the adults would tie our faces with a rag when we got sick.

Time passed by, and in the late 30s, we moved to Bibb County. I was still too young to go to school, but I started school the next year. By that time vaccinations came out and everybody in the county had to have one. The government scheduled special days for every family in the different counties. The people assigned by the government to give us the vaccine shots would meet the children at the school. After that, that old measles virus took a toll, and then came malaria fever. One of my brothers came down with it and became very sick.

There was a lady in the community that told my mom about this plant that would help us. It grew in the cow pastures. We called it bitter weed. We went to get the plant, and mom boiled it in a little kettle, and she gave him a glass full to drink. The remainder of it, she put it in a tin tub to bathe him in it and he got well. Back then, people believed in herbs, mainly because they didn't have money to go to a doctor. People had to rely on one another and have faith in God. Let Him fight your battles.He said, in the book of Revelations, "there is a tree that grows twelve manures of fruits and the leaves on that tree are good for healing and natural, believe it." As time went by, another disease called Typhoid Fever hit our community and took a toll. The government set up clinics all over the community and as the '40s took shape, more vaccine shots came.

Under The Cover

The World went to war a second time, in our community, some went to war, while others went to find work. That's when dad left, leaving my other brother, and me to run the farm. We were about eleven and fourteen years old at the time. We didn't have a chance to go to school unless it rained. The rest of the time we had to plow and catch the mule, right along with the grown men in the community. Sometimes it was dark in the barn, but we had to catch them. He had to come out, it didn't matter how he came out, head or tail. We would not have eaten any breakfast and sometimes it would be hours of plowing before mom would get breakfast for us. We would sit on the plow beam and eat. When we get through, we'd go to the well and drink a belly full of cold water. Then go back to the field and plow that mule crazy. You know the Bible states that there will be seedtime and harvest time. We had tilted the land, planted the seeds, and we would have to leave the rest in the hands of the Lord. Now it was time to sit back and watch it grow. We'd be relaxed doing nothing until the harvest time period. We boys in the community would roam the woods looking for swimming holes. We'd run up on a place with a big hole, we'd call it the Blue Lake. The water was so clear, you could see the bottom. We would go by the watermelon patch, and every one of us would get a watermelon. We get to the water hole and throw them in. We did not have swimming trunks; we'd get in naked. We would swim for about an hour or two, then we would eat the watermelon.

Under The Cover

Nobody made us get out of the water. We would each start grabbing watermelons and saying that my watermelon was bigger than yours, and saying, "no it ain't, mine is bigger than yours." Of course, a fist fight would start after we finished eating the watermelons. About that time, it would be about four or five in the afternoon, time to get the cows to the dairy and milk them; feed the mules and slop the hogs. Then the sun would go down, we'd go home to eat. It wasn't always what we wanted, but we ate it. Buttermilk, crackling, peas, greens, hog jaws, ham hocks, sweet potatoes, or anything to make a meal. On Sunday morning, we mostly had chicken for breakfast and lemonade. For dinner, we would have stew meat, rice, string beans, and iced tea.

Summer was all gone. Work would start again. We would plant the seeds, we water the seeds, and we watch them grow. Then comes the harvest time again. The first thing that's ready is cotton picking time. Everybody in the house in the month of August went to the field, even the old big "Tomcat." You look around, there he comes up like a cotton roll dragging a sack during harvest time.

Come Sunday, there wasn't any plowing or visiting, everybody knew most people go to church and have a good time singing and praising the Lord at either one of the two churches in the community. Cotton picking when revivals would come, we'd go to church at night and the moon would shine just like it was the day. The adults would put the young children in the front and give us boys and girls as teenagers a chance to walk about three steps behind them. Every once in a while, one of the mothers would say, "you all are alright back there?" The girls would say yes ma'am. Revivals were always a good time to socialize. Since it was dark, us guys would walk the girls home, even if we'd walk past our house. Some of the parents would let us stand on the porch for about five minutes, but the door had to be open, and you had to talk loud enough so their mom could hear the conversation.

About this time, we were halfway through picking cotton, and now peanuts shaking time. It lasts about a week, and then back to the cotton picking. About the middle of October, we were done picking cotton and it was time for corn. We had to break corn after corn, sweet potatoes, and then pick peas. Sometimes we would run upon a rabbit and everybody in the fields is trying to catch that rabbit. Sometimes he would get away from us. It was an old hawk that always sailed over the rabbit and then he would drop down and catch that hair on the rabbit. We would stand and watch him sail away with him, hoping he would drop him.

As the season passed, it would be time to pick peas and time for hog killing. This would be around the middle of November. Everybody in the community killed hogs, cooked lard, and made sausages. Man, that was some good eating. During this time, food was plentiful, nobody went hungry.

Come the middle of December everything is gathered as Christmas nears. We get a chance to go to school at that time. The school would be out for about a week after Christmas. We went to school in January, February, and part of March. After that, we went to work again. Life on the farm is just like a circle round and round. We lived in that community for a long time and that was the lifestyle. Then the plantation owner died, and we moved. Dad began to rent a farm, he started farming for himself, just as he did for the other man. After about three weeks there, a man bought the place and we had to move again.

At the new place, we caught pure hell as the land would raise dust; the one mule we had, dad had to sell to buy food for us to eat. At that time, I was halfway in the eighth grade and had to drop out. My older brother had married. All of the Hubbard men moved out, left home, and made a life for themselves in the city. Dad couldn't find any work and one day, there was a man cutting logs and he asked dad about me working. Dad told him that I was going to school, but he would talk to me. So that evening when I got in from school, he told me about it, and I stopped school and helped to support the family. I had to stop school because there were no jobs available. People didn't offer you anything to eat, so after that truck of timber ran out. We were out of work again. So, when I heard about the Navy Ordnance plant hiring, I went there and upped my age. I was going to be seventeen in

November, and I wanted that job. The lady asked me, "How old are you?" I lied and said eighteen, so she gave me an application and I took it home.

She told me to bring it back tomorrow and they will give you a job. I went home with no knowledge about filling the application out. There was a girl down the road from us, who had finished one year at Georgia Baptist College. She filled it out that evening for me and that next morning turned the application in. The lady at the office did the rest of the paperwork. I was hired and worked there for about eighteen months, making sure I helped support the family and took care of myself in the process. Unfortunately, at the end of the 18 months, I was laid off. I now had no job or education to speak of.

I walked around for a long time without a job. One day I thought about going to the unemployment office, so I did, and they sent me to Macon Iron and Paper Company. I worked there for a while. At the time they were building the Armstrong Cork Company and Papermill. When it was completed, I quit Macon Iron & Paper Mill and worked there. I worked there for about four years and got fired. I was on the street again. During this time, the Korean conflict started, and the Navy Ordnance Plant started hiring. I was lucky enough to get a job again. I worked there for about six months and was drafted into the Army. I served two years and upon returning, I went back to the Navy Ordnance Plant and worked there until it closed down. They transferred me to Robin Air Force

Base where I worked for thirty-seven and a half years. I retired in what is called the service time period. I left the base on June 22nd, 1985.

Let me tell you about my social life. I have never been in any sort of trouble. Being brought up the way I was, earning what you got was important; I worked all my life, and never begged for anything. Back in those days, you either had it or you didn't. Nobody gave you nothing; I take that back, nobody had nothing to give you. After things got better, all of us boys were almost grown. We all got jobs. My brother and I even bought a car together. On Sunday evenings we would get our girlfriends and go to the airfield and take them on an airplane ride. We did this every Sunday; it was our thing until one Sunday the girl I was dating had to go to church with her aunts. That gave me a chance to take another girl, she didn't like that at all and told me as much. Some of these girls' moms found out and would fuss because they said the plane could crash and kill us all. They told us, we "better not ever get in a nether airplane." Of course we still were able to slip by and still fly. We were having big fun, but as time went by, my brother under me left home for Jacksonville, Florida, so that left me without a running partner.

Although I missed hanging with my younger brother, I was able to trot the globe. The guys on the job started calling me the Globetrotter. Somehow I still managed to have a social life and was dating this girl in Florida. Back then people wrote each other letters, especially those that were dating, and she wrote me one. I remember this part when she said, "I went up on the mountain and I fell down on the ground--the hardest fall I ever had was when I fell in love with you." After trotting the globe for a while, I decided to settle down.

I already had my eye on the girl I wanted to marry, so we got together. I knew she was the right woman, and she knew I was the right man. I proposed and she said yes. We've been together for 50 years. These many years I was supposed to have had at least six wives. Fifty years with one woman that's too long to stay dead. That's almost as old as I am. Time passed and different things happened like wars, rumors of wars, and even the weather.

God didn't promise us all sunshine without rain, or cold without hot. So now it's time for people to change, I am going to move on to what I am trying to say.

I've talked about different things. People change, we talk about integration. We never had that problem until we moved to the city. We talked together, always played together and we lived next door to white people, but we didn't go to school together. They rode the bus and we walked. The ones that didn't know us would pick fights. What's crazy is after seeing that we wouldn't fight back, they'd come and play with us. We had a secret place to meet under the shed where we would play. One of the white neighbors had a big tricycle. I wanted to ride that tricycle so badly, but they said I was too big to ride.

They would let my brother stay and eat because he and the white boy were about the same size, I was too big. I knew what time it was, time to carry my black ass home.

Back in the day, you could play with the boys if "that" girl was outside. Their parents would call her in the house, because they didn't want us around her, they didn't even want "that" black girl around the white girls. If anybody told me that one day, black boys and white girls would be marrying here in Georgia, I would have said, no way. I would not have believed it. I would've asked him "are you crazy?" I would ask guys with white girls if they were crazy. They would laugh and walk away. My son would say no dad, they have been doing things to our women ever since slavery, now I am going to pay them back. I have a nephew and a cousin that have white girls and they have children from them. I ask them, "boy, you all ain't afraid of the little children running around calling me Uncle Hubbard?" The little children smile and say, "Hello there."

Black girls going with white guys. I remember back then it was a black woman living in the community and every man, white and black was having sex with her. I was small but I knew what was going on. The married women in town called her the winch. What broke this one man, he went there early one Sunday morning, and he had a little white dog. His dog followed him everywhere he would go. This time, his wife followed him. About the time he got settled down, the wife knocked on the door. The woman in the house answered, "who is it?!" The man's wife called the woman's name. The woman in the house said "I'm in bed." The wife replied, "my husband is there too." The woman said, "he ain't!" The wife responded, "yes he is because his dog is laying on your porch."

Back then they did have deadbolt locks. The wife knocked that latch off the door. Her husband hit the back door running. After the women fought, the word got out in the community. The woman in the house had to move. Her name was Aunt Lily and she moved to the city. The white men wanted to know where Aunt Lily moved to. The jokers sure tried to keep up with her. She must have had one of those comeback things that the men couldn't get enough of. One day we were walking down the big road. This cracker rolled up beside us and asked my uncle if he knew where Aunt Lily moved to. My uncle told him he did not, back then you didn't tell anybody anything. White or black.

It was a white woman with her husband living in the community. He was much older than she was. At night she would come down through the quarters looking for a man. It was a man thing. The first black man seeing her, that's who would get it. One night her husband played smart, he followed her, and went back and rounded up every white man in the community. On that night, I heard that truck coming, and I saw all of those lights. He had to catch that ass wagon. I mean he didn't stop in Macon like Aunt Lily had to slip around different places. When he got a chance, he went to New York. Those white men grinding Aunt Lily didn't have to go anywhere but back home. Black men have always caught hell, even about their own women. Back then, all white men had the advantage on the black man. Now the little black boys are paying them back.

I always heard what goes around comes back around. What goes around your back, buckles in your belly. He (the white man) used to kill someone about his woman, but now she is just another woman. It seems like another world. Black boys, white girls, white boys, and black girls. I don't know what this world is coming to. Think about this, the guys go off to the military, in the service, and go to Japan, China, Korea, and all over the world. They marry those foreign girls and bring them right back here to America. That's why I say it will never be the same. These babies from Germany, calling them "brown babies," the black and white, they called biracial. I don't know what they will call them when they start cloning them. There will be no more human race. No sister or brother, just a mother. That's so sad. In the future, if someone wants to get married, who are they going to marry?

Okay, that's enough. I want to take you back to Aunt Lily. She said she stayed away for a long time. I was finally in my teens. One day this white lady was in town, and she saw Aunt Lily downtown. Aunt Lily had gotten old and gray, so she moved back to the country to be a nanny. She took care of that lady's children; she was too old to screw. But when she was young in her prime, she screwed every man that had a dick. She didn't care what color, all she wanted was the dick.

After she moved back to the country, I heard another woman tell my mother one day, you know that old slut moved back down the road. She is with her missy; she is taking care of the children. When Aunt Lily was young, she was a good-looking, brown-skinned woman. She had long curly black hair and a nice shape. I was too young to screw, but I could look at her and my little man-hood would get hard.

After she moved back to the country, she was too

old for me. At that time, I knew men would kill their wife. This man is in the field plowing an old Joe tipped up through the woods to get him a piece. I remember back in the community; this old man had a young wife. He loved to go Coon hunting at night, so one day he had a bunch of Coon dogs and went off and the dogs got out and went down through the woods near the back of his house and started barking. It used to be a sawmill. My daddy was back there on the sawdust pile working away. His wife and another guy sitting on the porch. The other man told him your dogs are barking like they have found something. Yes, it was my daddy and his wife. You talk about a rolling stone; my dad was one back then.

Back then, there were some good girls and good

women, and there still are some further down south of Macon. Sofkee used to have some pretty women. That's where everybody would meet on Sunday evening and play ball. Sometimes they drink liquor and fight. Those crosstown rivers want to be bad from Walden and Avondale, straight bullies. They didn't have any shit for us Sofkee boys. We didn't have cars like the boys of today, we walked or rode bicycles. There were only two black guys in our community that had cars. These guys were big time niggas and did not mess with them. Not too many white people had cars, but they had farm trucks with all that dirt on them.

Going back a few years, I remember the first piece I got you. Talking about feeling good, I never had it before. I told my brothers about it and we all laughed. Boy, I wanted some more of that sweet thang. I started getting it pretty regularly, slipping through the woods and across the field any way I could get there. All I wanted to do was to see that girl again. One day, dad told me and my brother to cut firewood. I spotted her going through the past going to the store. She was just waving at me; my brother didn't see her, but I told him I'll be right back. My dad came up and I wasn't there. When I did get back, it was "hell to care the captain!" But it was worth every lick he gave me across my back, my girl made me feel good. Dad spoiled the whole damn thing. I was intending to brag to my brother about it, but dad broke that bragging up with an ass whipping. I was a big old boy, but dad didn't give a damn. He required us to "do what I said, when I say it." He didn't care about us proving our manhood with these girls. We boys caught hell a lot.

We had good times as well as bad times, but through it all, we made it. I am proud of the way I grew up. There was love in the house, not only in the house, but also in the community. As said earlier, we didn't go to school that much, but we knew how to say "yes, ma'am," and "yes sir." It didn't kill me or hurt me. Of course, with time everything changes; people, style and we don't eat the same thing anymore like we used to. It's alright to eat pork chops two or three times a week, but give me some steak and gravy or sometimes a piece of ham. Even the style of clothes has changed, sometimes I want to put on short pants because I get tired of the long ones. Nowadays, you learn to just listen and make your way through the world. You don't have to have a master's degree from Howard University or a Ph.D. from Yale. All you have to have is a little common sense. I had never been to college; I didn't even finish high school. I think if a man can talk to God, the Most High, he can talk to anybody. When you go to some places, you have to have an appointment, but with God, you can talk to Him anytime and anywhere. Amen.

To make it through this world today you have to know how to fight and sometimes you have to know how to run. It's another world and a new ball game. I got in one fight; I was afraid of him. He was always picking on me, he knew I was afraid. So, every day he would hit me just as hard as he could. One day my girlfriend and I were walking through the cemetery lot, and he spotted us. He came running right up in my face. I tried to go around him, but he blocked me. I got a chance, so I broke and ran. He caught me and started beating me. My girlfriend called out, asking me if I was going to just let JR hit me like that. I was just standing there. My brother Charlie saw us, and he said to me, "Junior you better hit that boy back. If you don't, I'm going to tell Daddy." When Charlie said that, I don't know where that strength came from, I hit that joker so hard, I knocked him down and he rolled like a log on the graves. He got up and ran back up in my face, I drew back to let him have it again. He was a little ole black- hard looking joker, but after that day, I didn't have any more trouble out of him. From that day on, he was my buddy.

EPILOGUE

This story has never been told about a family of nine boys and three girls. One nephew, one cousin, all live together in a four-bedroom house. I remember back in the year of 1930 we lived in Houston County on a big plantation. They grew vegetables, peaches, and sweet potatoes. We had plenty to eat. In the late 30s my dad moved the family to Bibb County to another plantation. We raised everything; my dad and the owner raised hell a few times, but overall, they got along okay. As time passed by, dad decided to take on a sharecropper part, so we stayed on that farm for a while longer.

So, in the early 40s, we moved again. We all had grown up. In December 1941, the US had entered World War II after the bombing of Pearl Harbor. My oldest brother had to join the Army, so that left my next brother, dad, and I to run the farm. At that time, I was only twelve years old, and my brother was fifteen. We both had to take on men's jobs. We didn't have a chance to go to school like the other boys and girls. The only time we did go was when it rained, because we couldn't plow, pick cotton, shake peanuts, or break corn.

Under The Cover

I remember after the war in 1945, the order came down from President Truman for every boy and girl in America to go to school between the ages of six to sixteen. I was glad, yes Lord. I went to school a little longer then, but I had to drop out and get a real job. They call it public work, cutting logs at four dollars a day from sunup to sundown at twenty dollars a week, which was big money back then. I had to help take care of the family. So as time passed by, I was lucky enough to get a job at the Navy Ordnance plant, which paid sixty-five cents an hour. I was making more money than my dad. I told a lie to get this job. I was only seventeen, but the job required me to be eighteen. I wanted that job and I got it. I worked there for about fourteen months and then I was laid off.

As time went by, I got hired at a paper mill making eighty cents an hour, big bucks. I worked there for three years. About this time the Korean Conflict started. I was lucky enough to go back to work at the Navy Ordinance.

I am Herklee E. Hubbard, Jr. I was born to Mr. and Mrs. Herklee Hubbard Sr. on November 18th, 1929. We were a family of twelve. I am sixth out of twelve children. I had a rough time growing up. I stopped school to work in the field. I didn't have time to go to school, I had to work. The day school opened, one out of the family would go on that day and the other stayed to pick cotton and shake peanuts. Long about December, all the crops were gathered, then we went to school. A little while after Christmas for two months out, again plowing and planting. Goodbye school again.

If I had a chance like kids today, I would have been a lawmaker or a doctor. Children of today got a chance to be anything they want. The little time I do have, I know how to get through the world. I have never been in any trouble. I remember it was one lady living in the community, her husband died, so I started working for her from sunup to sundown for fifty cents a day. That mule didn't stop until 12:00 o'clock. I would go home and eat; the walk was about a mile and a half. About the time I got home and ate, it was time to go back and catch old Bessie until sundown. About 3:30 the school children were out; they would come down the big road. Now, I've always been a cool cat and this girl came from the city to the country to live with her aunt. So, when it rained, I had a chance to go to school. This girl out of all the boys, she picked me. She wrote me a letter one day and gave it to my sister to give to me to read. I remember it by not looking at it. I will never forget this part. It says, I went up on the mountain and I fell back on the ground, but the hardest fall I ever had was when I fell in love with you. Boy, when you get a letter like that, I became a Rolling Stone. As time went by, things changed. We fell on hard times, no work, there was nothing but farming.

FUN MEMORIES

Herklee Hubbard, Jr

Under The Cover

www.ingramcontent.com/pod-product-compliance
Lightning Source LLC
Chambersburg PA
CBHW020308010526
44107CB00001B/31